One Paycheck and A Housewife

Home economics on a small budget

By Kate Singh

Author of *The Homemade Housewife* and *Living on One Income*

Katesinghsite.com

Coffee with Kate on YouTube

Contents

Chapter 1

Preparing to live on one income...or just being broke.

Many of us have daydreams of large homes in tree lined neighborhoods where all our neighbors' wave to us as we drive by in our fully loaded compact minivan. We pull into our driveway with the green lawns and flowers lining the yard. We enter a large foyer and see stairs winding up to all the large bedrooms for all our bright children, then make our way down a long hall to enter our sparkling kitchen with all the gadgets and stainless steel. Sigh. We have our husband help us unload bags of groceries from the Whole Foods down at the local town center with all those organics and grass-fed beef. Life is grand. Oh, wait, that was just a commercial.

When we plan our wedding day we plan on success in all areas, we've seen the commercials, we have them imprinted in our brains. We will live the dream! We'll be loading that new washer while wearing our cute jeans. We will be having fabulous dinner parties with a big bar b q smoking in our big backyard and that music in the background, "Come on over to my house, we can have a good time..." or something like that.

This may be a reality for some, but for most of us, this dream gets us into massive debt and sometimes foreclosure. In the end we may be living in a tiny apartment grilling some discount meat on a small charcoal bar b q on the balcony while avoiding collection calls on the phone.

That dream could very quickly become a nightmare.

Building a good life takes time and work. It's best if purchased slowly with cash or savings. But things happen no matter how we plan it all out. One partner loses a job, one of you gets pregnant and then wants to stay home even though that wasn't the initial plan, an injury on the job, health issues, or you just want one person to stay home, but money is so, so tight!

I genuinely support any couple or partnership where one person wants to stay home even if there aren't children involved. A housewife or househusband is a luxury and pleasure, and if they are good at their position, the family is fortunate indeed. And sometimes a partner is at a job that is soul-sucking and needs to quit. Or you adopt and want to be there to support these new family members. There are so many reasons for one person to stay home that goes beyond the traditional homemaker or children in the house.

And, sometimes it happens unexpectedly or quickly.

So, how do we have this luxury today? Can we really afford to have housewives or househusbands? What is the reality of it and will it create constant stress meeting those bills? Are you all doomed to poverty with only one person working? Will the bread winner need three jobs?

So many people are going back to this model and making it work despite the housing cost on the rise, gas, and food being more expensive, and those pricey little children. Families are making it work because the quality of life is so much better when a mother or father stays home. It can save the home money in the end if done correctly. Not to mention the sanity and balance of a home and its members.

However, there are sacrifices and, depending on where you live, it might be big ones. The family would need to be open-minded and surrender a bit to the process and what may need to be given up to reap the benefits of a life that will, in the end, be much more fruitful and satisfying than all the iPhones and Smart stuff out there. The family may have to downsize the large home or relinquish a fancy car. Homeschooling may be the only option. Living in a town a bit farther from work or buying that run down home and learning home repair. This is a new age and requires new creativity to make it.

You may have to learn a whole new way of life. You could possibly love it.

I'm typing this soon to be book, on an old 300 dollar laptop that my husband, quite proudly, did some repairs on this afternoon with black Gorilla tape and a bike pump to blow out all the dust in the fan. I'm drinking homemade espresso out of a white cup my spouse purchased cheaply at Target on sale for our son's birthday party because we didn't have enough dishes and I hadn't time to hit the thrift store. I live in a charming blue cottage that is small according to most standards today. There are often too many people and critters in my bed, and we miraculously make it with one bathroom. I have had to put my office in the laundry room and convert the water heater closet into a pantry for my dry goods. This is my reality. But it is the best life I've ever lived thus far and I love every day of it!

Now, I make light of it for some laughs, but I know it may depress some of you and you're reaching for a bottle of wine right now to get through this book. However, remember that there is always a silver lining to all clouds. Is that how that saying goes? Ah well, there is hope and true happiness found in these pages. You may even see the true meaning of life by the end of it.

Today my family lives well, and we own a sweet home. We eat delicious meals, dress nicely, wake up happy, go to bed satisfied. However, recently there was a change in my husband's work, and we have had a significant curtailment of funds. I am working with a smaller budget and little grocery fund. I haven't had to pay attention for a long time since we had savings and abundance. This happens. If you don't pay attention, you look at your accounts one day and gasp in horror while clutching your chest.

Ah, but I've been through this before, and to me, it is a challenge. I know how to have fun with it all. I pull out my old books on frugality and thrift by my wise mentors and, with pen and notebook in hand I draw up a new plan for my family's financial expenditures.

This year I have learned and practiced the art of frugality more than any other time in my life, and I'm enjoying it thoroughly. If anything, it has improved the quality of our lives. We don't run about eating fast food and find ourselves busy all the time. We have learned to entertain ourselves at home, and I'm learning all sorts of new homecooked recipes. We have created a home that is efficient and inviting with our own hands, and there is even some homesteading happening.

We don't live on very much, but I feel like middle class without all the stress. We don't worry about recessions or housing market crashes. Our life is set up to withstand any changes that may occur.

I would love to invite anyone to come along and see if this seems appealing. Maybe learn to just live on less or maybe downsize your whole life.

Our history

Bali and I started out financially stable when we married. We did a wedding on a budget. It was lovely with a garden ceremony and twinkle lights and dancing in a grange hall. It was all done under $5,000 and that included wine and rings. We had catering, a DJ, and a little honeymoon right across the street from the Circle K where Bali was a manager. I would have been irritated, but the Inn was very nice and overlooked the ocean, but everything did in that town because it all *was* on the ocean.

So, we had no debts, one car that was paid off, decent rent, a roommate, two jobs. Life was starting out with incredible financial abundance and stability.

Now, our story isn't like most. We didn't buy the big house with the massive mortgage during the housing market bubble, we married years after that. We weren't young kids paying off painful college loans, I had already done that. We didn't run up piles of cards buying new furniture and eating out all the time as newlyweds or purchase new cars. We already did all that in our past. We both married later in life and had made all the financial mistakes and paid for them. Now, we had experience and some wisdom. When I became pregnant, we started living on one income and putting the other check away in savings since we already had an agreement that I would stay home with the baby when the time came. I used the roommates share as grocery money to feed the whole house (roommate included), and we ate from home, packing lunches, and so on.

We made little mistakes such as buying the fancy new furniture to look more grown up even though the house was decorated just fine in old furniture I had inherited from my mother. We bought far too many items preparing for the baby, most of which we never used after Arjan arrived. We had no idea life was going to change and fast, requiring a move and some serious frugal living.

After Arjan was born Bali's boss partnered up with a slick slickster and the running of the gas stationed changed terribly, as in money was disappearing, gas and groceries were no longer arriving, and within the year the station closed, and Bali was without work and with a wife and infant. Our town was tiny and work was limited. Fortunately, we had money in savings, and I had seen the signs on the wall and started a daycare. We were blessed with a large family that needed my daycare as much as we needed them and with my daycare money rent, bills, and groceries were paid.

This went on for half a year, and then an old friend from Bali's village called and offered him a job managing his gas station/market. We were so relieved. But it was in Walnut Grove in the Sacramento area, three hours from my beloved ocean and forest.

Off we went and settled into a ranch house in a pear orchard on the Delta River. A new life began. The job was not a management position but rather a cashier job for $10 an hour. Bali worked long, hard hours for the next two years and I raised two yummy little boys mostly alone except for Alice, my elder neighbor, the only one near me in 600 acres of pears. I felt much compassion for my husband working so much, and I was cautious with the funds. I had learned a trick or two over the years such as grocery envelopes and budgets, but I needed to learn more, much more if we were to make it on a bit over minimum wage.

Enter stage left, the librarian. He was a small man who loved to show a new gal a trick or two on how to really work the library system to their disadvantage. I had always thought you only could get books that were in the library, so to learn that I could get online and order in different *towns*...different *counties* far and wide! I became the queen of ordering stacks upon stacks of good, enjoyable, free fiction. Amish fiction. I developed a fascination with the Amish and Lancaster County and all their ways. I would sit outside in our large yard with the levee road between us and the large river on the other side. Under an unusually large olive tree, I would consume books on Amish life while my little ones rolled about in the grass or on blankets. I was fascinated with their slow-paced, simple life. The Amish are very good with money and make almost everything by hand. They are hard workers and devout to their beliefs.

Then I discovered The Complete Tightwad Gazette. I don't know how, but I found it and purchased a copy on Amazon for a few dollars. When it arrived, I read it from front to back. I was hooked on this frugal life idea. When Amy Dacyczyn talked of having a large family and purchasing an old New England home in the country while living on one small Navy income of 30K a year and saving money, I was hopeful, to say the least. She talked about being a new housewife with her first child and discovering daytime talk shows. On one of these shows, the audience was complaining of how impossible it was for a couple to get into the housing market or how a family could only afford two children. She decided to prove society wrong and onward she went to master frugality and thrift. She and her husband saved $49,000 in less than seven years on this single income and purchased that pre-1900's New England home in the country.

When she wrote this, it was in the early eighties. Here I sat in 2014 hearing the same exact complaints. I became obsessed with ordering piles of books on frugal living and watched homemaking vlogs on YouTube to add to my venue of home-based entertainment.

With some help from a childhood friend who lived in the next town over, we made vast buckets of laundry soap, I hung baskets of laundry on the old clothesline that was set up in the 1950's by previous farm tenants, and I picked all the fruit around the farm with permission. The old families had planted fruit and citrus trees about the homes. Alice and I would pick the fruit and enjoy. I even tried my hand at baking bread and then I ordered Dump Dinners from a TV ad and set about learning to make cheap and simple meals one dish meals. I had my grocery envelope, and I used it earnestly. We lived 30 minutes from a town of good size and ran errands and grocery shopped only once a week. That helped more than I realized. When you can't go shopping daily, it helps with the temptation. Also, when you forgot something on the grocery list you couldn't just go the next day and get it. This prevents excess shopping. We all know that going to the store to buy "one item" does not happen. You often leave with a few more bags of "must needs".

I did not grow my own garden or learn to can at that time, nor did I keep making bread or laundry soap, but I was learning.

Time went on, and things got better as they often do. Bali went back to work for the old boss who owned a station a half hour from us. Though his commute went from four miles to an hour drive, he made better money and worked in a much-improved environment. Around that time, I was becoming curious about homeschooling, and somehow that led to learning about decluttering and downsizing. I decided it was time to move back into a town where I could walk around with the boys and find a smaller house, so I wouldn't spend all my days cleaning. Our ranch house was big with two living rooms, three bedrooms, and two bathrooms, not to mention all the yards. It wasn't that expensive and had been the only house we could find at the time, but it was far too big for us.

We found a tiny two-bedroom house of 800 square feet in the town of Sacramento and cut our overall cost by $600. It only took an hour to clean the house and three minutes to mow the lawn and not all of Bali's one day off to tend to the backyard. Back then Bali worked six to seven days a week, so if the family day was spent mowing vast yardage, it was a bummer. The commute was cut in half, utilities and rent were significantly reduced, and I could push the stroller and later pull a wagon to five different parks, a big yellow library with a rose garden, and two large grocery stores.

During this time with all I had learned, and now all this extra time on my hands, I started a writing career. I added blogging a year later. That was the beginning of a love affair. I loved writing and blogging, and it provided a fantastic outlet for a woman who was often on her own with her two boys. I had left behind my community back in Fort Bragg, CA and was home alone with a husband that worked from 10 am to after 11 pm all week. Writing saved me. It would also make some side money in the future, but not for a long, long time.

With the extra money we saved from downsizing I traveled with my children, bought sliced bread and convenience foods, and spent hundreds at the thrift stores. After years of being on such a strict budget and being so isolated, I lost my frugal ways. The lesson here is this; if you are too extreme for too long, you will lose your stuff the minute some extra cash flow happens. There must be a balance. But we will get to that later.

Through all the ups and downs with the money flow, we still did not touch the savings that had survived all these years. This was the savings we built when we were both working and before I retired to be a full-time housewife. We still had the dream of buying a home. But now that we were ready...the market was back to the pre-housing market crash of 2008. Housing cost were doubling before our eyes and rents were on the rise by 13% a year. I was truly nervous. I would pour over all the real estate articles and feel my face flush hot and my heart pound. I read about homelessness on the rise and families making up a large portion. I worked at a soup kitchen, Loaves, and Fishes, and saw people with children in the lunch line that were living on the river. I was scared.

One day I started the venture to find us a home. The problem was that we only qualified for a small 130K loan and even the most ramshackle house in a lousy neighborhood was at least 150K and going up fast. This was Sacramento were housing was considered cheap still. Not for long.

A small town to the rescue

Around this time Bali's boss had promoted him to manage and fix up a run-down gas station in Yuba City, 30 minutes from where we lived. Bali fixed up the gas station/mini mart and was getting to know the locals. I had been to the town in the past and was confident it was definitely NOT our town. I had fantasies of forest and charming towns, an old fixer upper with a large garden and hens pecking and scratching about the front yard. Yuba City is known by some as Uglyville and was for many decades. It had two highways running through it and had been ravaged by meth years ago. It was a town in need indeed.

But as I drove about the paved over, run down suburbia's of Sacramento's forgotten parts to find junk yards for homes, as I started to feel claustrophobic by the 1.5 million people in the city, as I began to dream of small towns and friendly neighbors, I ventured to Yuba City and beyond to find us something, anything...a trailer on land, a small shed with a yard...I was desperate. And this town of Yuba City began to show me its more charming parts, its tree-lined neighborhoods, and some affordable homes that just needed TLC. I started to feel drawn to the town and made offers on a few run-down houses or nice houses in run-down neighborhoods. I thank the sweet Lord for looking out for me and having all those deals fall through.

If we waited a couple more months, Bali would have two years working with the same company, and we would qualify for 200K instead of just the paltry 130K. After being outbid a couple times and me being very dramatic about it all, we decided to wait for two short months.

But one day I had that feeling. You know that inner guidance that whispers ever so softly? It was time. We didn't qualify for the big loan yet, but my intuition told me that what we wanted was a cheap fixer-upper with a small mortgage. We have been through work insecurity in the past, and I wanted two things for my family; for Bali to work much less and have a quality of life rather than just a worker bee, and a mortgage that was smaller than any rent we had ever had. A mortgage so small that if the breadwinner lost his job, he could flip burgers and still pay the bills.

I brewed a pot of coffee and warmed up the laptop, determined to meet this challenge. One search led to another, and in the end, I found a humble, worn out, exhausted, abused 1941 fixer-upper that was currently a bank owned HUD house up for bidding. I bid on it along with another very stinky and filthy house that day, and the next morning I was the proud owner of the stucco 1941 home. It cost 135K.

Now, why did I tell you this very long story of our journey? I love telling this story, *and* it is a teaching story with so much more to come.

What I had learned so far was this; when you marry and are sure you would like a family, more than likely one of you will want to stay home with the infant or children. Not everyone wants this, I understand, but most women I talk to do want this very much and because of debt and big mortgages, they can't. It is sad to see this happen to a family. I want to help. We have had times of very little income and no income and did just fine, however, we were prepared and did this preparation before we had our first child. Saving as much as possible, being debt free, living simply.

Today we are going through work and money challenges again, but it doesn't seem so hard because we were prepared again with buying this cheap little fixer-upper, staying out of debt, and I have become more frugal and thriftier than I ever thought I would.

If we make financial decisions today with the future in mind, a future that might have job loss, a recession, a housing market crash, disability, an illness, and all sorts of situations, we will avoid hardship on a mass level.

Live small. Live simple (I'm not talking minimalism at all). Live debt free or get out of debt as fast as you can. Have savings that will get you and your family by for months if not a year. Live with the understanding that the economy, the housing market, the job security is very up and down. Be prepared for the down so you can enjoy life no matter if it's up or down. You will be unphased as a family. You may even be able to use rough economic times toward your advantage. Many wise souls have become wealthy during recessions. Think of all the first-time landlords years after the housing crash? Four years after the bubble burst, properties were extremely cheap.

There are wiser souls with more significant experience and years more practice, and I will share these people, books, Channels, and blogs to help inspire you on this journey. We are going to have some fun here, I love a good money challenge and to make a game of it. I've learned some balance to not lose my mind and wallet when the money is flowing richly through our accounts. I'm still learning how to squirrel away those acorns for the long and cold winters. I have plenty to share at this point, especially after a good year in this house learning about bringing an old home back to life, gardening, canning, making my own cleaners, devotedly making bread and cooking from scratch. I have gone back to crocheting gifts and decorating on, literally, a few dollars. I have learned so much this year along with really using all I learned all those years ago living in the Pear orchard. I still have The Complete Tightwad

Gazette by my side, and I've added much more to my bag of tricks.

Mostly, I've learned to have a lot of fun and be creative. Let's brew up some coffee or tea and have a long chat on how to save money, live on one small paycheck, feed the family well on a food stamp budget, and make as much of your cleaning products and food from pantry ingredients.

This won't be a big novel, more a booklet to get you started and inspired. If you find you need much more to work with, I will have references along the way and at the end of the book. I will go over fundamental ways to start saving, cutting cost, and even paying off debt if that is what you need to do. But for more details, schedules, recipes, and information I have other books **The Homemade Housewife** and **Living on One Income** that are packed with everything you need. I also have a blog and YouTube channel where you can join me in my home and learn all I'm doing and still learning to save money and live a stress free and full life with my family.

Chapter 2

Eating for less than a latte a day

Let's start in the kitchen. One of the fastest ways to get your money situation under control and make a significant change in the budget is with the grocery bill. There are three areas we spend the most, I heard this the other night and agree; housing, food, and transportation. There is also shopping, credit cards, and entertainment.

If you want a real money boost and fast, this is what we do; stop eating out or buying lattes at Starbucks immediately...like tomorrow.

Then we assess our pantries, cupboards, freezer, and fridge. I find that cleaning and organizing my shelves and pantry helps me discover items and foods I had forgotten all about.

Organize by food groups;

- Pasta, rice, and beans.
- Crackers, bars, and snacks.
- Soups and canned food.
- All things to do with baking, flours, sugars, chocolate chips.
- Seasonings and sauces.
- In the freezer have meats on one side and veggies on the other, maybe convenience foods in the middle.

The next thing to do is make a menu from all you found in your kitchen storage. You can start with a week or two. Try to work with what you have and then make a small grocery list of extras you may need to round out the dishes. See just how long you can go on your pantry goods.

Start making all the coffee drinks in your kitchen and invest in a To-Go mug or two.

Find a binder you may have stored away (to start collecting menus) or at the thrift store and begin the habit of menu planning and pantry inventory weekly, bi-weekly, or if you feel brave, monthly.

America's Cheapest Family, by Steve Economides, is an excellent resource in learning how to save and cut the grocery budget. They are a family of seven with the mother staying home, they used to live on an income of $35,000 a year, and Mrs. Economides worked with a $350 monthly grocery budget to feed five growing children, three of them being boys. They have a book all about this, *Cut Your Grocery Budget in Half.* You can get both books at the library (because we just don't buy books anymore, right?). There are some books I do love and reference so much that I buy them cheaply on Amazon or find at thrift stores to add to my library.

Ways to save money on groceries are looking for sales, cutting coupons or getting coupon apps on your phone, planning weekly menus, and always going to the store with a grocery list in hand.

Another few tricks I've gone back to doing are going shopping at the crack of dawn without children and without the spouse. I eat breakfast and take my mug o' coffee and shop before the masses arrive. Just me, the roosters and the rising sun. I love it! I can really take my time choosing the best sales and do the math.

Having a grocery envelope is crucial. Choose an amount that is realistic for your family and divide it into four weeks. It may help to put the money in four separate envelopes. This will be for groceries, toiletries, cleaning products, and dog/cat food.

Start finding those coupons. There are so many online coupons now. I am just looking into this world of coupons so you may want to look up a tutorial on YouTube.

Don't shop hungry. Or sleepy, thus the To-Go mug of coffee or tea.

Buying bulk and perimeter foods

Buying in bulk and the primary food groups are money savers. Learning to cook from scratch is easier than one may think, it's also a creative endeavor.

I order 25 to 50 lb. bags of beans, lentils, rice, flour, and oats at a time and store them in 5-gallon buckets with tight sealed tops.

I buy fruits, vegetables, eggs, meats, and soy milk.

Seasoning is also in the bulk bins.

Olive oil, dish detergent, and coffee is purchased in gallons or 5lbs.

I only shop at two stores; WinCo and Smart Foodservice Warehouse. This was after trying out every store in my town and within a 30-minute drive of my town. It came down to these two being the cheapest and offering the most in the way of bulk and healthful foods.

A snapshot of my shopping day

I rise early, 6:00 am, and shower, dress, brew my coffee and have a quick breakfast of no-bake oat bars I learned how to make with *Do It On A Dime*. It is merely peanut butter or any nut butter, oats, maple syrup, and anything else you may like. I add unsweetened coconut flakes and dark chocolate chips. You heat the peanut butter, and maple syrup or date syrup then combine the ingredients, stir well and mash them in a pan. Put in the freezer for a quick chill. When they are hard, you cut up and eat. Yum. I fill my mug with coffee, Truvia and creamer and pack my grocery bags, look over my grocery list and head out. I love not having the boys because I can really turn up that radio and sing or talk to myself. I love those boys something deep, but a little space does me good.

I reach WinCo with the sun rising and the roosters crowing. Literally, Yuba City is filled with wild chickens, and WinCo is the most popular poultry hang out partly because many of the elders, especially one elder woman in particular,bring them water and food daily.

I shop leisurely, spending most of my time in the produce and bulk section. They are right next to each other. I may take a tour down the coffee aisle and get the cheapest coffee. I love to check out the canned food isles for deals or Hunts canned spaghetti sauce that is .99 cents. Pasta is often less expensive in bags then bulk. You need to do some math with bulk and bags by adding up the weight and dividing the price. I bring a calculator now.

I hit the meat and eggs, the soy milk, grab some doggie biscuits because my dogs were my first children and need treats as well. I make one last check on my grocery list. Oh, see, I forgot frozen vegetables. I will load up on big bags of the vegetable medley, peas, and corn. We are done, and after checking out, I bag my own groceries, another reason it's more affordable at WinCo. Without children running around like wild puppies, I can bag quickly and move on.

I may do one other store, Smart Foodservice Warehouse. It is a restaurant supply warehouse. I get a gallon of lemon dish detergent for $5 and buy huge bags of onions, garlic, potatoes, coffee, rice, and so on.

I do some shopping at Briar Patch Coop in Nevada City on Fridays. I am a member, and I truly love this store, but it's costly, so I just order bulk organic grains and beans and coffee when money isn't as tight. Right now, we have a goal of rebuilding our savings, and so I sacrifice our health a bit with nonorganics since they don't fit into a grocery budget of $350 per month.

What about toiletries and dog and cat food, you ask?

We buy tissue in bulk, soap in bulk, and I buy big bottles of shampoo cheap and use for them as shampoo *and* bubble bath. They last forever. I have found big bottles of Suave at Smart and Final and just stock up. We buy big containers of Coconut butter at WinCo and use this to cook with, make popcorn, and keep a jar in the bathroom for our face, hands, and bodies. It last forever. My husband likes a manly Dial soap, but I use Ivory, I get a pack for a couple dollars, and it's so mild I can use it on my face, and the children, as well as the body and it can even be used to make laundry soap.

For dog and cat food we go to our local Grange Coop and purchase a 40 lb bag of Diamond brand for $32 for Maggie, the cat. It lasts all year. It may not last as long since I seem to be feeding the neighbors cats lately. They eat junk food at their house and crave the healthy meal. I can't complain because Maggie goes over to their home in the evening to eat a junk food dinner.

For the dogs, I mix the high quality and expensive Taste of the Wild for dogs with Diamond brand that is less quality but a good brand and far less costly. This stretches the food a couple months and totals $80. I feed my dogs as much as they like, keeping their bowls full, but Clyde and Babu are not ones to gorge themselves, so we have always done this.

What can you do with boring foods

Our cupboards and pantries look so dull and for the person on the American diet, they would cry with despair trying to find a snack. In our house, you need to build and bake and create all the dishes from scratch. This does not mean that I don't indulge in cheap, packaged food. I'll get to that.

Here are some ideas for the foundation foods in our pantry:

Flour wheat and white flour can be used to make tortillas, bread, both grain and Amish white bread. Flour is used to create basic white sauces and even those cream of chicken or cream of mushroom sauces. Pancakes, waffles, and muffins, cakes, cupcakes, pretzels. How about homemade pasta. If you want to make egg-free pasta, you'll need semolina flour.

Potatoes I could eat potatoes for days and not get bored. My favorite for mashed or the yellow potato, they are richer and creamier. I used small red potatoes for potato salads and smashed potatoes. Idaho is the cheapest and are used for French fries, baked and loaded potatoes, potatoes au gratin, hash browns, and cooking up a batch of fried potatoes with loads of onions and bell peppers.

Rice and Beans, it can be as boring as that, or you can make burritos, casseroles, slow cooker meals, skillet fajitas with the addition of a little beef, enchiladas, tacos. You can use lentils to make lentil loaf. Rice to make fried rice. Black beans can be used to make chocolate black bean brownies.

Oats There is the good old oatmeal. I also use oats to make oat flour for black bean brownies and lentil loaf. I use oat flour to make pancakes.

Bananas I use them for banana and peanut butter snacks, smoothies, and banana ice cream. There is also banana bread or muffins, healthy cookie recipes, pancakes with the oat flour.

Now we just need to start cooking. If you are new to cooking or need to refresh yourself on the topic, I found some great Channels. I know I refer to YouTube often, but I love watching tutorials and learning from others by seeing it done. The only cookbook you really need for a foundation is *Joy of Cooking.* Everything else can be found online. *Taste of Home* is one of my favorite resources and right now I love *Brother Green Eats* on YouTube. They will show you everything from learning to shop and make amazing meals on the same amount as a coffee a day to food prep for a weeks' worth of cooking. They even teach you how to make your favorite fast foods from scratch in your own kitchen. Who doesn't want to learn how to make Taco Bell dishes? *Pasta Grannies* is another place I go for pasta making lessons on YouTube. *Two Shakes of Happy* does a great video on meal prep for the week. If you are into the plant-based and trying to lose weight *High Carb Hannah* and *Chef AJ* are fabulous. For vegan try also *It Doesn't Taste Like Chicken.* There is another channel that is so delightful, *Great Depression Cooking* with Clara.

Basic seasonings

You need foundational condiments, and then you build from there as you learn new recipes. The basics that flavor food and make so many things from scratch tasty are;

Oil, salt, pepper, vinegar, soy sauce, garlic, and onions. Maybe a tobasco or sriracha. Later you can add dried soup packets such as Onion soup, taco seasoning, Italian seasoning, and so on.

Lately, I've been buying garlic and onions in bulk because I sauté everything in them. I buy bags of frozen vegetables and sauté piles of garlic and onions until caramelized and then throw in the veggies and cook until they are grilled. A bit of sea salt and you have a very delicious side dish to compliment those creamy yellow mashed potatoes.

Some extra seasoning I have in my cupboards:

Chef Merito granulated Garlic powder or Chicken seasoning

Knorr Tomato Bullion with Chicken Flavor and the Chicken Bullion

Colman's Mustard

Ground Cumin

Smoked Paprika

Old Bay Seasoning

Roasted Garlic powder

Toasted Sesame Oil

Gebhardt Chili Powder

Spike Seasoning

I was really into veganizing our favorite dishes for almost a year and collected a lot of good seasonings I still use. There are many dishes I still prefer vegan style to the original meat or dairy based way now.

Meat as a condiment We were vegetarian for almost a year. We do this often, vegetarian or vegan for a time and then off. Although we have gone back to meat at this time, we use it sparingly, and I cook many vegan and vegetarian meals in between.

I won't compromise on clean meat, and I try to be as cruelty-free as possible. We buy hormone, antibiotic-free chicken, free range eggs, and grass-fed beef. I was happy to discover that WinCo is now carrying all this along with more and more organics and vegan alternatives. Yay 21st century!

A whole chicken will be baked up with lots of Chef Merito seasoning and then it lasts all week because I section it up and use it for a casserole, burritos, enchiladas, skillet dishes, or/and soup. You can also save the carcass and cook it down with left over vegetable trimmings to make a stock to freeze for a later stew or soup. Waste nothing.

A package of grass-fed beef will be divided and used for a couple of batches of spaghetti sauce.

Fish is maybe once a month or twice and small pieces sauteed with tons of onions and garlic.

Filling the plate and the bellies Filling bellies is much more than just filling them with food. We need food that is packed with nutrition and fiber. You can get a 50lb bag of potatoes at some food warehouses for $10. Rice and potatoes are filling and nutritious no matter what the new fab diet is. Frozen or fresh vegetables in season are also loaded with vitamins, fiber, and minerals. I fill the plates 3/4ths with rice, beans, or potatoes, and vegetables, 1/4th with a meat or meat substitute. You can also do huge slow cookers with soups or a pot roast and use mostly grains, potatoes, and veggies. How about a big bowl of stew or soup with hearty ingredients and thick slices of homemade bread? I'm thinking winter foods now as I watch our skies fill with grey clouds.

We can really go through eggs fast. I've taken to mixing in rice and veggies with my eggs, and it makes them last a week instead of two days.

Cheap packaged food to make the budget stretch

I sometimes buy the five pack of mac and cheese or Korean ramen. When I can buy five meals for .25 cents each, I will. But I add things. For example, with the mac and cheese, I'll sauté garlic and onions, along with frozen veggies and some canned chicken or tuna and add that for a very full meal with some goodness. With ramen, I'll add kale, spinach, carrots, broccoli, and maybe tomatoes. You can do this with Rice a Roni as well. Don't be ashamed to buy the cheap foods, they may not be healthy, but they are less than a dollar, and we are working on tight funds. You can improve the quality with vegetables.

I also buy generic brand whole wheat saltine crackers in the big boxes. These are good for cheese and crackers or peanut butter and jelly on crackers for the children during snack time.

Asian, Indian, and Hispanic markets

We can drive over to Sacramento and hit the big Asian supermarkets to load up on fun foods. Here in Yuba City we only have a tiny Philippino store and one very dark and dusty Korean store. I love this Korean store despite its lack of a good housecleaning and how greedy they are with the lights, turning on one more bulb wouldn't cost them that much, for goodness sakes, I could see better! They have cheap rice noodles of every size and shape. They have Pho bouillon and Won Ton bouillon and big bags of mustard greens. And they have my favorite Korean ramen that is so darn good that American ramen will never suffice again. Once you go Korean, you never go back.

We have a lot of Indian stores because this town is 20% Punjabi. We can find Indian seasonings and black channa (black garbanzos) that you can't find elsewhere. Bali loves to cook his Indian food and buys all sorts of Masalas.

We have a La Superior a few blocks from our house and I love this store. It's a bit worn around the edges but scrubbed clean, bright lighting, and loud Mariachi music. I spend more time shopping just to hear the music. They have fantastic prices, and you can get all sorts of ethnic Hispanic foods. I purchase packages of tostadas, love their white potatoes, cans of Café Bustelo espresso, and the bags of cinnamon sticks for my stove top potpourri.

I find that the Asian, Hispanic, and Indian stores are far cheaper, and you will be introduced to exciting new foods. Try it out.

What to drink on a budget

I don't buy juice, milk or soda. We buy some soy milk for cereal and coffee or a smoothie, but even smoothies are too expensive right now. I use the soy milk sparingly. We have a Brita filter on the sink and a Brita pitcher in the fridge for cold and refreshing water. Coffee, tea, and water are all we drink. I was putting juice in my boy's water or those Vitamin C packets to flavor, and they had a ton of cavities this summer. We are back to clear water. It's a healthy habit to get the family into, and you can add mint from your container plants or we use lemon from our neighbors' tree since our trees are too small still. In the summer I use lemon and stevia for lemonade. It cleanses the liver and kidneys. Hey, a refreshing drink that cleanses the body?!

Cooking from home, brown bagging lunches at work, and making thermoses of coffee will save you so much money that you will be inspired to take other steps to improve things.

Chapter 3

Zero spending and cutting cost

Putting a kibosh on the spending altogether for short periods of time help to jump-start saving or get the family budget under control again.

You can go for a month or a season. Some try a whole year. So, what is this zero spending? I was introduced to the idea of zero spend for the month by Ruth Soukup. This concept may have been around longer, especially during the Depression Era, right? But it's popular now with this addiction to consumerism running our finances into the ground.

We are in a season of zero spending, and it's taking some time to adjust. It's harder when you know there are funds available. Much easier to do when nothing is available and there is no choice. But to build our savings, we must "pretend" we have no money and just pay the bills.

A zero spend has no hard and fast rules. You pay the rent/mortgage, bills, commute cost, and food and nothing outside of that. Some people who choose to do this for a year or more will add things they can't do without such as new books or travel, maybe eating out once a month or a weekly mocha at the cafe. There are emergencies and must haves. You can figure out how you want to work it and how long. I will say that it really does get the household back on track, can save a lot of money fast, and helps to break the habit of shopping and spending mindlessly. You will savor that mocha when it's only once a week and not daily. You will appreciate the smallest things like never before when you don't glut on them constantly.

Our biggest issue is spending on groceries. The other day I looked at our accounts and was shocked to see that the secured card I have through our bank was overdrawn when I had been putting money on it to pay off. Where the heck did all this money go? I scanned the last month, and it was all grocery stores. We had gone on tour trying out all the stores around us near and far to see who had the best deals and never left their double doors without a few bags of food and products. Our food budget is beyond trouble. I'm now following my advice from the previous chapter, and all is well.

What to do for entertainment

This is what I do, personally. I write out the budget, cut anything we can or reduce it. Recently I switched to Xfinity for a better price on Internet and got rid of cable. We purchased a very generic Smart TV that only gets YouTube, Netflix, and Pandora. There are some random and strange channels on there as well, but all we use here are the top three. Our entertainment bill is now $7.99 for Netflix streaming on the big Smart TV instead of $130 for DirecTV that was loaded with infomercials and movies I didn't care to see or couldn't watch with children about.

From the garage, I rustled up the HDTV antenna I purchased through Amazon years ago. It just plugs in, and you stick the square rubber piece to the window. I moved the smaller TV in my bedroom, and now I get 27 free channels on a good day. I'm thrilled with those old westerns, the old movies when color was new to film, 80's sitcoms, and local news (I try not to watch that). In the winter there is nothing cozier than curling up on my big king-sized bed and watching those old movies while crocheting a scarf.

We don't get PBS, but I found all the PBS cartoons; Sesame Street, Dinosaur Train, Sid the Science kid, and so much more on YouTube.

Another thing we couldn't get on DirecTV or cable were Indian movies. We get Punjabi movies, other foreign films, and Korean dramas on Netflix, YouTube or online.

I'd say, for us, getting rid of cable was the best thing ever.

We have another item that cost a bit more but is so worth it and will never be cut from our budget even if I must get extra babysitting jobs. It is the Yuba City Racquet Club. This club is private and has been around for decades. It is very nice with indoor and outdoor pools and Jacuzzis, saunas, steam rooms, tons of exercise classes and rooms upstairs and downstairs filled with new and old equipment. It is a beautiful place, has a little café area, friendly staff, swim lessons for the boys and a daycare that is amazing! This daycare is in a separate house with a huge backyard filled with trees, forts, toys, outdoor climbers, swings, houses, and on and on. The inside is filled with toys, kitchenettes, bathrooms, and a kitchen. It is free for three hours a day.

I have never, ever had a daycare or place I could leave my boys without one of them having a hard time with the separation. I have no babysitters, and the father works all the time. This daycare they love so much that if I come back early, I get sour looks from both boys. I take my time reading a book on the treadmill for an hour or exercising on the stair climber while watching people play tennis on the courts out the huge bay windows. I can swim laps and steam my whole person, take a class, or weight train while listening to my favorite songs that I've collected on my SanDisk (I know, so outdated, that's me). In six years, I've never had this time, and it is saving my sanity and bringing joy and balance to our home.

In the summer we would all go to the health club and swim in the outdoor pool for hours. We made friends, and the boys had swim lessons. There was always a lifeguard. It was something we looked forward to every afternoon when dad got home.

Vacations and travel are not in the budget, so this club has given us so much pleasure and something to do every day if we get bored or just need to get out of the house.

The cost is $160 which breaks down to $1.34 per person per day. When I investigated our local public pool for the summer, it was $5 per person for only two hours. With the health club, it can be all day. We can come in the morning and then in the evening after supper. And to have three hours of daycare a day is beyond a dream.

These are significant ways we stay busy and happy. Then there is the library which every frugal article and book will repeat. However, what some libraries offer that isn't mentioned is a program called Zip Books. Not all states and libraries provide this program. However, you could always see if they'll start. With Zip Books you have them order you any book under $35 off Amazon. The book is delivered to your door, and after you've read it, you give it to the library. If you take care of the books, since you receive them new, the library is happy to oblige you as many books as you like...one at a time, of course. I had a medieval series I was hooked on, and the library had only one of the seven books. I was thrilled to discover this and was able to order and read each book. The books are popular and cost from $7 to $15 each on Amazon. It was the *Age of Faith* series by Tamara Leigh.

Another thing I realized with the library is that I can order movies I can't find on Netflix or YouTube. I'm cheap and won't pay extra for the DVD's to be delivered. I'm devoted to my live streaming for $7.99, but sometimes I want a movie for the kids such as Mary Poppins or The Wizard of Oz.

Oh, I forgot one more luxury. This is educational but cost a bit. It turned out to serve us all so well. My sons attend an outdoor school on Fridays for a few hours in Nevada City. It's called Fox Walkers or 4 Elements Earth Education. It is three hours in the forest running, learning about nature, animals, and Mother Earth. Our eldest has made so many friends, and they both love this day so much. Bali and I now get a Friday date day for a few hours and can shop, go hiking in that gorgeous forest, or have tea in the Briar Patch Coop café and talk uninterrupted. We can hold hands and stroll leisurely without chasing a little person down every five minutes. We are also making new friends through our sons' new social life. We did some play dates this summer with parents of Arjan's friends, and it turned out we were all perfectly matched and bonded fast. This is such a treat since we left our community by the sea years ago and have moved from town to town and experienced a lonely and isolated life for the last five years. Now we are rebuilding a community here, and my heart feels full. Can't put a price tag on that.

Nevada City is a beautiful mountain town with lots of hiking trails and charming places to play tourist. It's half an hour away and serves as that getaway place when I feel the travel bug but have no money for this desire.

Homeschooling is another great money saver. The one child is homeschooled, and Sam is close behind him. We signed up with a Charter school and they alote $2500 a year to each student. They also lend Arjan a laptop. All his curriculum is paid for, books he finds interesting on Amazon, and Fox Walkers along with other outside enrichment classes such as music, theater, cooking, karate, and so on. Before the school year begins, we meet at a store called A Brighter Child. This store is loaded with wonderful curriculum of all kinds and imaginings for all grades. We shop for all our school supplies, and it's paid for right then. Pens, paper, books, games, programs, puzzles, equipment...all paid for.

My son is thriving and works at his own pace which is advanced. He can also choose what and how to study and follow his passions without falling behind. We always have the support and guidance.

For a family that has no money, this is an answer to it all. In public schools, parents must buy all the supplies for the year. Here it is all paid for, and there is no getting up early and fighting over getting dressed and shoving down toast. My son isn't in school for 6 hours, away from his brother and me and then coming home with hours of homework. He doesn't encounter bullying and constant testing.

Is he socialized and up to date? Yes, he has playdates with other homeschoolers, and we visit friends and family. We go to parks, the health club childcare or what they also call Kidz club. He is far beyond his first-grade lessons. Sam has started his schooling on his own accord, I have them both do ABCMouse.com which I do pay for, but it's $50 a year and so worth it. The program goes from PreK to third grade now. It covers math, English, grammar, reading, writing, social science, geography, and science.

So, we have covered the entertainment and education, the travel, and now you may want an overview of what a budget looks like and how we disperse our money.

Foolproofing the budget

I'd like Bali to take over the finances and just hand me grocery money monthly just like in the old days, but he won't. I can be like Jekyll or Hyde with finances. I'm either hardcore penny pinching and feel like I'm training for the Olympics of frugality orrrr...every nickel is burning a hole in my pocket.

We all have good intentions and goals that sparkle and shine. Then we have our personal saboteur that lives upstairs in our head. We make a budget and then see that the local thrift store is having a sale and it's 5 dollars a bag of goods. We can't pass that up! Heck no.

I'm having issues this round with the not spending gig, so I had to foolproof things. This is what I did.

- I made out our budget. It is pretty bare-bones at this point. I have Bali only deposit that amount that is needed to pay the mortgage and bills.
- All the extra and over time is deposited in a separate bank we use only to build huge savings. Our family bank is Wells Fargo. Bali had a US Bank long before we met and so we turned it into our savings haven. I am joined with him on this account in case something happens, and I must access the account, but I smartly refused a debit card. I don't even look at the bank as I drive by.
- Grocery money is in an envelope at the beginning of each month.
- I use my royalty money that is automatically deposited in our accounts to fill up secured credit cards (Bali and I both have one) and the household savings. Soon I will also receive money from YouTube since I monetized it and that will also be used for savings. When everything is filled up the extra will start going to the US Bank savings.
- I deleted my account information and credit card information on Amazon and PayPal. Not that I can't be trusted...
- I gave my credit card and debit card to Bali. I'm in a retraining process.

Some bills are automatically withdrawn and some I pay on BillPay. I can't touch a penny in the accounts because there is always something going through. I like to cushion it a little to protect from overdraft.

I use my babysitting money as cash in my wallet, and I'm trying to grow it, so my purse always has at least $100 tucked away. There is something that feels extravagant about having that much in one's wallet. I rarely have $5, but that is about to change.

Ways to save on the bills you do have

We can save on groceries. We can save on utilities. We can save on insurances and commute.

This is how I'm learning to save on our utilities as of lately. We used to be on SMUD, and it was so cheap compared to PG&E, which is our power company now. We are on a CARE discount program for now, but I don't want to depend on it. We want to thrive not live on discount programs. Recently a young man came to my door and offered Solar. I welcomed him in but didn't hope for much as I had already been abandoned by two previous companies. They said they couldn't match our bills. I'm pretty good at saving energy.

This is a sort of new but thriving company V3. They install and maintain the panels and make money by using your house as a sort of energy garden to harvest and sell power back to PG & E. We pay them to use our allotted amount. We met with them several times and felt it was a great situation. We don't have to buy the panels, and if anything goes wrong, they fix it all for free. They take care of everything as long as we want the solar. It will be 104% offset with an increase of 2.4% yearly which beats the 10 to 20% or more increase

PG&E does. Our bill will be around $95 a month compared to the $140 most months. Without CARE it would be $230 a month. Also, PG&E will be increasing rates and changing billing cost to times of usage, so it will be going way up. Last year and this year we've had terrible fires in Northern and Southern California, and some were blamed on PG&E pole wires. They are in for 15 billion so far, and it was just decided in the courts that they could offset the cost by increasing rates. This means trouble for many and bills they may not be able to afford. I'm relieved by this new marriage to V3.

Water rates keep going up as well, but I gave them a call today, and we only have two more years of rate increases. I understand it takes money to keep our water clean and pay for the workers and pipes. I did find something fantastic out while quizzing the office lady. We are given 15 units a month, and we are only using 7 units monthly even with my big kitchen garden out back and the 12 fruit and nut trees, the lawn in the front and all the flours, roses and shade trees. If you water wisely, you just don't use much.

- Use grey water where you can. We use the boy's tub water on the lawn. We use the clean water from a bucket we put under the faucets when we run the water to heat it up for a shower, on container plants. We take short showers and never leave the water running.
- Once my garden veggies are sprouted and getting strong I only water every 3 to 4 days unless triple degree weather and then every 2 to 3 days depending on how they look. This encourages the plants to grow deep and strong roots.

- We water the new fruit and nut trees and grapevines two times a week, but we soak them deeply.
- We use a lot of mulch. This can be wood chips are straw. You can buy a bale of straw for $10 at the feed store.
- I only do laundry once a week and have an HE washer.
- We don't flush continually. It never smells terrible as we only a skip a few flushes, and we drink water like crazy, so we don't have strong odors. This causes much debate when I post it on YouTube.

As for heating and cooling the house, even with this new solar we still must pay for gas in the winter.

- We had some weatherization done through the PG&E Weatherization program, but we have tube and knob wiring, and no one will insulate our attic. There is about 5 inches of the blow in insulation up there already, but upon further investigation, we have decided not to insulate further. It could be a serious fire hazard.
- With our tax returns last year, I had an attic fan installed. It helps so much. Our bill was as low as $65 some months this summer. But it also wasn't so hot this year.
- We have double pane windows, but you can use thick flannel curtains to keep the cold out and the heat in.
- I use substantial area rugs on our cold wood floors in the winter and have warm rugs in the bathroom and kitchen on the cold tile.

- I will be using a Presto Heat Dish from Costco to heat our main two rooms this winter instead of wasting hundreds on gas to heat a whole house and rooms not being used. A friend used it for her home last year and said it saved her a hundred a month on her utility bill. With plugins, you must be careful, they can eat up the electricity. I have yet to try it out.
- You could always buy an AC window unit in the winter when they are cheap and use in the summer instead of central air. It saves hundreds, literally. I want one so badly, but Bali won't give in...yet.
- We all wear warm slippers in the winter and go barefoot in the summer. We dress according to the seasons. Shorts in summer, sweaters in winter.
- The thermostat is set low but comfortably. I like being warm. We turn it off at night. I like the house being cold and snuggling under quilts. I put flannel sheets and extra blankets and comforters on all the beds in the winter and in the summer, we do cotton sheets and a thin bedspread.
- In the summer it needs to be hot to bother us. I think we're all part lizard. We keep windows open and fans going. I just close doors, windows, and blinds on the sides of the house where the sun is currently blazing down. We have planted some shade trees around the house. However, that will be some years before we reap those benefits.

I think that covers most things here with savings. There is still garbage, but you can't reduce that bill. You could get rid of it. We used to recycle or compost everything we could and throw the rest of the garbage at Bali's work. They had huge bins, and we really have very little waste especially without diapers. It's just the dog poop that gets gross. There are ways to build composting buckets for doggie doo. I've seen it. We may do it! We have a lot of yard waste with all the trees, and we need to have that disposed of. Everything else is composted.

We have Vonage for the house phone since we have family in India, UK, and friends in Canada. It's $28 a month. Our two cell phones are $50 for unlimited texted and talk with MetroPCS.

Bali works less than a mile away, and the kids and I walk almost everywhere. We live in a perfect location to walk to the Hispanic grocery, Raley's, four nice parks, the library, and even the clinic and dad's job. We save on gas that way. I have a wagon I pull along and pack food and ice water and if a boy gets tired he climbs in for a ride.

We have free insurance because we are low income right now and I lowered our Life Insurance from $130 to $43. We will still be taken care of if one of us expires. Cars are paid for, so insurance is basic and low. Plus, we don't drive much, and work is close, it's $55 a month for two cars.

There you have it. I think we covered everything in this arena.

Chapter 4

How to afford beauty and clothes on a budget.

I don't get manicures or pedi's, I don't frequent the beauty salon. My husband did my hair this last time after four failed haircuts in three years. I don't shop for clothes often and we don't go out to eat. What do I do to not get depressed? A lady needs some pretty dresses, a nail polish, or to not cook every day, right?

First, I'd clarify that we are not always on a no spend and I've had many moons of thrift shopping. Going out to eat with a six-year-old and four-year-old is more painful than fun. Our idea of eating out is the dollar menu at Taco Bell and last Friday Bali, and I had a dinner date alone at Taco Bell for under $10 that we scrounged up in the truck along with change in our wallets because we failed to pack food and were starving while waiting for our sons at Fox Walkers.

The last haircut I spent $80 on something that looked nothing like the photo I handed this hairdresser lady. A few months ago, I had Bali shave it all off because I had tried to fix it and then I had died it a few odd colors to try something new. My hair was fried and weird. Then I looked like I was recruiting for the Army, so I just wore a hat for weeks and now I can wear my headbands and look fun.

Build your own beauty salon

I do all my own beauty treatments at home. In the winter I do glycolic peels, and in the summer, I just wear a lot of sunscreens. I do my own pedicures and wax my own legs with Nads.

For a nightly routine, I use a washcloth and lather with Ivory soap, warm water, and cornmeal to exfoliate. After rinsing well, I put on Retinol Serum 2.0% by EveHansen that I ordered from Amazon. I apply liberal amounts of coconut oil and use my DermaWand. In the morning I rinse my face thoroughly with warm water. I only wash my face at night to get all the sunscreen and dirt off. I apply more coconut or Shea Butter on the face, use my DermaWand and then lots of sunscreens if working, walking, or playing outside.

In the winter I'll do 30% glycolic peels by Youthful Glow also found on Amazon. You must be careful not to use retina or retinol with this, or you'll burn your face off.

For makeup, I only use L'Oréal Double Extend mascara. I love this stuff, it has on one end a primer and the other end mascara and makes your lashes very thick and long even if they aren't naturally. I use some lipstick, and that is it. I have issues with my mascara smearing all day because of all the coconut butter and sunscreen oil. I recently discovered if I applied a generous amount of cornstarch to my eyelids and lashes, my mascara stays put all day and doesn't smear or wear off! I feel brilliant and don't even want to know if this is an old trick, I just want to feel special for a moment.

Bali trims up the hair for now, and I'm just growing it nice and long and natural, grey hair and all. I apply coconut oil to it daily, and it's getting thicker and healthier. Bali shaves his head since it's bald and shears the boys as well every six months.

Clothes, glorious clothes

As for clothing, I completely rebuilt my wardrobe over the summer. I decided I like dresses after all and I wanted to look good as I go on in my years. I shopped around online at Walmart, Dress Lily and other discount online stores choosing great dresses for my shape and size. I rebuilt a wardrobe with dresses long and short, short stretch pants, long, cute shirts, and colorful headbands, along with bras that hitched up the melons and attractive and comfortable lace briefs that stayed in place. I think I spent around $200 to completely redo my wardrobe down to my sandals. Before I wore frumpy t-shirts and loose pants. My clothes were getting stained and worn, and it was affecting my self-esteem.

I began rebuilding the wardrobe and taking on a beauty regime shortly after a woman at the library asked if my sons were my grandsons and when I said they were my children she seemed doubtful. I am in my forties, but please! I was looking a bit haggard so I realized I needed to do a make-over inside and out. Just imagine those movie montages with the motivational music in the background. I threw out the old frumpy clothes and in came the long summer dresses, boxes were being delivered daily for a time there. I bought the black sandals, the earrings, and started the beauty regimes to revive my grey skin, the cute short hair grew in, and bright headbands were donned, the berry and dusty rose lipstick was applied. I also changed the way I ate, increased my water drinking, and went back to exercising daily. Hello pretty lady! It didn't cost much, and your confidence is a priority. You don't have to do it all at the thrift store. I love the thrift, but sometimes a lady needs new clothes. I even got myself a new bathing suit 1940's style that I saw in an old movie.

There are many discount stores, and if you know your style and size, you can do it all online.

But it was short-lived, and now I'm delighted with my closet and won't be shopping for years except a little addition from a thrift store now and then.

As for the man, he has tons of nice clothes from his bachelor days. The boys have bins and drawers and closets full of nice clothes. Most of the clothes were hand me downs from friends who have older kids and took much better care of their things. With the boys, I update shoes and clothes as they grow and with them in Fox Walkers, I did need to buy snow gear and rain gear. So far, they even have snow jackets from the hand me downs.

A word about hand me downs. Don't turn them down. My husband would disagree as he has had to make a few deliveries to the thrift store. However, we have some lovely furniture, and the boys have been nicely dressed from top to bottom and all seasons for three years now. All on hand me downs. When people know that you will take things off their hands, you get some great stuff. And not so great stuff. But you pass that on and bless others and donate to the Goodwill.

Once we were given a few huge bags of clothes left behind from a friends' tenant. Most of it was junk, but I found warm, nice thermal shirts for Bali and me during winter. The gas station gets very cold, and he needs these. I pulled some plain, dingy cotton undershirts from the pile and dyed them tangerine for a dollar and some cents. I had four summery looking v neck T-shirts for working out and house cleaning. I also inherited a sturdy laundry basket just as my white one fell apart, and some nice jeans. The rest went to a thrift store, and a pile of nice, warm coats went to a homeless man.

Chapter 5

Cleaning the cost-effective and efficient way

I had a friend who was on such a tiny fixed income, she was on disability and raising two children on her own, yet she always had a clean and tidy home, scented candles glowing and full decorations for the holidays. There was always a spread on Thanksgiving and Christmas, and her home always looked cozy and inviting despite the old and worn furniture. I learned a lot from her.

I learned that it doesn't take much to make a home look inviting and charming.

An immaculate and tidy home is the biggest is the cheapest thing you can do to have a beautiful and presentable house. You can make your own cleaners and laundry soap for very little, and I like to get my ingredients in bulk as well.

- Baking soda
- Vinegar
- Borax
- Zote soap or any soap

That is all you need if you are tight on cash. If you want washing soda, you just bake the baking soda for 20 minutes. Lemon can help make scrubbing paste for sinks and tubs with the baking soda.

Vinegar and a bit of dish soap in water are what I use to clean windows, floors, and counters. Use a little oil to polish furniture.

I use these ingredients to make a laundry soap (and a couple other ingredients, but you don't have to use them). I get my laundry soap recipe and tutorial from *Our Little Homestead* on YouTube, and it's *Janie's Best Improved Laundry Soap.*

I buy a gallon of dish soap for $5 at Smart Food Service, a restaurant supply store. It may be wiser to spend a bit more for Dawn because it lasts far longer since you can water it down being that it's very condensed.

I use a broom and steam mop. My vacuum is bagless. I can wash out everything and never have to buy bags and rags. I use old rags to clean with and wash rags or old wash clothes as a dish rag. I never buy sponges.

You can even wash your floor my hand with rags if you have no mop or steamer.

Many ladies like to refer to *Flylady.com* for a routine. Grannie says to get *Side Tracked Home Executives* for a thorough year-round organizational system. I'll be getting this at the library soon as *I'm* not sidetracked.

I've only been fully employed as a housewife for six and a half years and still learning. I look up ways to do laundry, get whites whiter, get the tub unstained, seasoning cast iron pans, and anything I'm failing on.

We will talk laundry in a minute but here is how I do things lately and it's working out great. I feel rested and organized.

First off, Grannie gave me a colossal calendar scheduler from JoAnne's. She had used some of the months but went on to better things, and I inherited it (a hand me down). At first, I said thank you and how nice but shelved it. As fate would have it, I needed this calendar. I was doing too much, feeling fried and spaced out. I watched a show on being organized and brought the out the calendar, a stack of colored pens and white out. I scheduled in every day. I watched some vlogs of women doing Flylady routines and started a before bed and morning routine. I can't tell you how much it makes life flow in this house.

Night time routine

Before we go to bed the kids clean up all the toys in all the rooms. We have big baskets and tubs to throw things in for easy cleanup.

I wash the last of the dishes, wipe down the counters and table, tidy up the kitchen and living room.

Prep coffee for morning and pack husbands' lunch.

We brush and floss. The boys have already had a bath.

I do my beauty routine of face washing, products, coconut butter, DermaWand and put on my nightgown.

We may or may not always read a book in bed. And after everyone is asleep, I may watch a tutorial or cooking vlog on YouTube to get menu ideas or learn a new trick in homemaking. I don't read as the lamp will wake the man and critters and I always have at least one child in my bed even though they have their own bunks. I use earplugs if you're wondering about the noise.

Morning routine

A clean kitchen and tidy house greats me in the morning, so it feels good rising in this home. I turn on my coffee. The percolator takes a long time, so I shower as it heats and perks. I lather on my oils and lotions and dress, put on a little mascara and lip tint, add an apron and feel ready for the day.

As the boys rise, I make all the beds, cook a breakfast of steel cut oats, pancakes, or eggs for them and pour myself a big mug of creamy, sweet coffee and sit down to look over my schedule and plan my day.

If it's housecleaning day, I will start by vacuuming and sweeping all the floors and then steam mop. The house is tidy from the night before, so I don't waste time with cleaning up toys and there are only some morning dishes that I put in a sink tub filled with hot, soapy water for the time being.

On these house cleaning days, I make something simple in the slow cooker or a pot of spaghetti sauce and pasta. I will make a plate of crackers with peanut butter, veggies, and fruit later for us to snack on but we won't have another big meal until around 3:00 pm when Bali returns home from work.

I dust furniture and maybe organize shelves as I go. I may put houseplants in the kitchen sink to water and feed if it's that time of the month for that.

The bathroom gets a good tub scrubbing with Comet and a brush as it's old and stained and it's hard to make it look clean. The sink gets a rag and Comet, the toilet gets Comet and bleach and cleaned inside and out. I have three males in the house, need I say more? All the bathroom rugs get washed.

In the kitchen, I will take Comet and scrub the counters and stove. The sink gets Bar Keepers Friend as it's the only thing that whitens it.

This is about it.

Monthly deep cleans

If I went coo-coo crazy with the deep cleaning all the time, I would have a sparkly house, *and* I would be nuts. I would have no time to play, read, write books...borrrring. But I do loves me a fresh, clean, and sweet smelling home.

I had a cleaning lady once upon a time. She only came twice and then disappeared. That was fine because the extra funds to afford her soon vanished as well and I had to put my royal life on hold and clean my own house. I did learn a thing or two from observing her. I tried not to be obvious but I would clean with her, and I was fascinated. She washed floors by hand, washed the blinds and baseboards, scoured counters, and even got my old, old tub white. I never did learn that trick, if I had known she would disappear, I would have asked or paid better attention.

I take two to three days every couple months or when the house starts to feel grungy, to really get deep. I wash under sinks, wash fronts of appliances and cupboards, wash shelves, baseboards, dust blinds, clean that part in the window sills where the window closes, and there is dust and died flies. I wash parts of walls with little hand prints and chocolate, doors, nobs, I pull out stoves and fridges and sweep and mop behind there. I wipe the chairs and dust and clean the sides of furniture, not just the tops and places that show.

Every six months or so I shampoo the area rug or rugs. We have two big dogs and a cat. Things happen.

Another thing that helps tremendously is not wearing shoes in the house. It grosses me out to see people wear shoes in the home and put them on the couch knowing they have tracked through the residue of dog and cat poop and urine, spit, and rotten food, drinks, and gum. I have a collection of flip-flops on the back stoop and front porch for when we are outside.

Laundry and whites

For the first in all my years, I finally separate my laundry. We don't have many whites, I avoid them, but I do lights separate, then colors, then darks, and then towels with kitchen laundry. I wash bedding alone, and rugs last with all the dirty rags and steam mop clothes. I add a half cup of Borax to the bottom of the machine, the load and a small amount of homemade laundry soap.

I found a recipe to get the whites bright again. It is a cup of vinegar, a cup of Clorox bleach, a cup of powdered dish soap, and a cup of Borax. You fill a sink with hot water (I boiled a few pots of water) and stir in the ingredients and the garments or towels and let sit overnight.

I make a five-gallon bucket of laundry soap that last almost a year and cost less than a dollar a jug. It works great, and I love making it.

I found the laundry soap recipe on *Our Little Homestead, Janie's Best Laundry Detergent Recipe Improved! On YouTube.*

The solution for the whites is found on: *Theunfrumpymommylife, how to easily whiten white clothes,* YouTube.

Chapter 6

Home Sweet Home and homesteading in suburbia

Buying a fixer-upper was my dream. Perhaps not my spouses, but he has learned so many skills and proved himself very handy and clever through the transformation of an old and tired home to one that smiles brightly.

Having a homestead in town was the other dream I had for the home front. I imagined myself in an apron canning with huge pots boiling and counters of colorful jars filled with sauces and jams, I saw myself kneading dough in the early mornings, throwing feed to my hens, and picking plump tomatoes from my vast kitchen garden. We would have a taste of country farm life right here in town.

All of this came true eventually, but not quite as I had dreamt it up in my head. I did do some canning this year. However, my garden was lush but unproductive. Our squash only produced two vegetables so that gives you a clear idea of our failure. I had to buy the produce from Sprouts to can and it was a stressful weekend of watching vlogs as I boiled jars and stirred berries. It was also very fun, and I bought eight cases of unopened Ball jars off Craigslist for less than $7 a case.

We did have hens, but in the end, I gave them away. The home has taken a full year of work to bring its luster back and get it just right.

We found our home and set about painting, scrubbing, mowing down years of weeds and bring back health to old rose bushes and trees that had been neglected for years. We then set about planting fruit, citrus, and nut trees, table grape vines, and in the end, we dug up the useless lawn in the backyard, fenced it in, and I began learning all about growing an abundant kitchen garden (and still trying to master it, I might add).

Along with the farming, we dragged home a free chicken coop, painted it yellow with the leftover living room paint, and I paid $35 for five rescue factory farm hens.

An umbrella clothesline was installed in the small cement patio and I set about kneading that weekly bread. I also decided to be vegan after seeing the state of the factory hens. However, the man and boys enjoyed fresh eggs often.

We spent the first year working very hard, a couple trees didn't make it and were replaced, a few hens passed with the year for various reasons, and then we rescued a lone hen at Bali's work to add to the dwindling flock. After a year I was down to two healthy hens, and one was brooding for weeks, and the other was lonely, so I sent them to a woman that had lots of land and a rooster. I, personally, feel that to have chickens you need a lot of space for them. Our yard was long but between a tall wooden fence and wall and felt so closed in, was damp and cold in the fall and winter, even spring. My hens thrived in the garden all winter but when put back in their yard, while I planted the spring garden, the ones that had struggled a little in health since being rescued declined a considerable. It was sad. They need more space than people think, and it's work to keep a coop and yard free of parasites and lice. I miss them and will definitely have hens again when we have more land. I learned so much for the next time.

I didn't get to can my garden this year but decided to learn the art despite this. I watched canning tutorials and found good recipes. After a day shopping at Sprouts for produce, I spent all weekend canning triple berry jams, spaghetti sauce, and dilly beans. Without a pressure canner I had to pickle the green beans but found a vlog teaching how to freeze corn without blanching. It just takes a little sugar and salt heated in water and added to a bag of corn.

I've taken up crocheting again and have made scarves for the boys for winter and my neighbor's little girl on her birthday. My next project is a quilt.

There is always something simmering on the stove or cooking in the crockpot, bread baking, sprouts in the kitchen window, and music playing on the radio atop the fridge. There is always something growing out in my garden even if the squirrel gets to it first.

Even if you don't need to do all this to save money, there is something so satisfying about all of it. Also, even if you live in a tiny apartment, you can homestead up a storm. You can dry clothes on a rack, do canning in your little kitchen, bake all sorts of bread, grow sprouts in a window, use grey water for the container gardening you have on your balcony, grow herbs in the kitchen window or counter. You would be amazed at how much you can do without land and your own home. How about learning to knit hats, make quilts, darn socks? Find an old sewing machine and set to making aprons. Making your own food saves money and taste better. Growing sprouts is much cheaper than buying them. Making your own almond milk is quick and easy.

If you rent and have a backyard, you can use as you please than plant a garden and some dwarf apple trees.

Our lawn was 80 years old and depleted of any nutrients. We have added some compost and aged horse manure we found at a horse stable a few miles from us. It has helped, but my soil still needs work. I'm cooking compost right now, and by the end of winter, it will be ready to enrich my soil. Coffee grounds, egg shells, and banana peels will help return balance along with more horse manure. We have another pile of that behind the garage aging for the winter. I have big hopes for next year.

Reading backyard farming books and watching vlogs helps, but you learn as you go. They say it takes around three years to have a successful garden and I see why. Most of it is building up healthy soil if it was a lawn for years, then there are insects and weeds. Or those darn squirrels. Beneficial Nematodes were suggested to me, and they worked great. I do use Snail pellets as well. I tried the cans in the ground with beer, and that just didn't work. I'm organic besides the pellets. I use soapy water solution for aphids, and next year I will plant plenty of marigolds around my patch of tomatoes.

Gardening is fun, creative and therapeutic. I also have a lot of bird feeders and houses, bird baths and in the spring the birds migrate and fill my yard with the most amazing, beautiful birds. We have planted plenty of flowers as well to feed the bees and butterflies.

A home should be a sanctuary, and it doesn't have to cost much. We did use some of our savings to recover this house. It took $15,000 to do all the work and pay a carpenter to help us. This is for fences, painting the inside and outside of the house, tearing up carpets, repairing plumbing, electric, doors, putting up blinds, and all the landscaping and gardening. We also painted the inside twice, once with a lead paint sealant and then with color. In actuality, we could have done it for far cheaper if we had to. The man that helped us was not necessary as we later learned how capable we were and how easy it is to learn things on YouTube. We didn't have to paint the outside of the house, and if we had just dug up the lawn from the beginning, we would have saved on all the soil and raised beds we built in the beginning. We could have tiled our kitchen ourselves or used a cheap linoleum.

I look back on our spending and see how we could have saved so much money through proper planning and not getting caught up in wants. That is what I want to impart to you. You can have an adorable home for very little and even free.

Our house is shabby chic, colorful, warm and fuzzy. Almost all my furnishings are from thrift stores and free from neighbors and friends. I have filled it with plants I grew from trimmings, books I bought for quarters at the librarys' Saturday sales. Our one luxury item was a king-sized bed that is a pretend Posturepedic. It cost less than a thousand new and was worth every penny. I love that bed. We have a couple of bedroom pieces we bought when we first married, and I regret them. I am the fondest of my various thrift, and garage sale finds.

Most of the plants and pots in the backyard were given to us, found free, or we bought off Craigslist.

Now we are really into saving, so we make do with everything we have. Bali has become very handy at fixing things. He repaired the bottoms of four chairs I loved, but the wicker bottoms had blown out. They were given to us from a neighbor when she inherited a new dining room set. He found a free sink cabinet and basin from Habitat for Humanity they were throwing away and installed it after watching a video on installing a sink.

To refresh the look in our home, I just give it a deep cleaning and rearrange the furnishings, rehang paintings, and pick a few bouquets from our yard. I have free roses year-round. When we moved in, we found several rose plants on discount and planted a different color for each member of the family. I now can pick a $30 bouquet whenever I feel luxurious.

Since we stay home most of our downtime, it's vital that the house is set up for entertainment and we all have our space and fun "things" whatever they may be. We don't have play stations and Xbox's or iPads. We do have books and a new stack weekly from the library. We do have our Smart TV with movies and shows and educational documentaries or cartoons. The boys have plenty of toys, a huge sandbox outside, bikes, and each other.

I have my kitchen (my happy place) where I try new recipes and bread, canning, or just getting it organized and cleaned. There is a big, old radio on top of the fridge and I can dial in my favorite Christian music or a Chico station that plays modern or 80's if I feel nostalgic. Sometimes I put my laptop on the counter as I roll out pasta and listen to an Abraham Hicks seminar. I have the whole house that I love decorating.

Then there is my garden I love watering in the morning and listening to my morning doves that took up residence in the Palm tree in the neighbor's yard behind our garage. They love the birdbath, and I feed them well.

Bali has his garage, and there are all sorts of work out equipment to exercise on, or he can repair furniture. He also has a green thumb and has had more fun planting all kinds of seeds and pits from his cooking. Bali literally cooks, saves the seeds and plants the next day. I never think it will work but he now has an avocado tree under my laundry room window and bitter melon is growing like a weed along the fence. I can test the soil, nurture it, do moon dances and pray to the Great Mother and barely get things to grow, that man throws out last nights dinner and has a crop. Am I jealous?

Bali loves working out there and will spend all day weeding, rearranging pots, mowing, and playing in the front and backyard. It's his first home and spending a whole day working on our yard fills him up with pride and satisfaction.

Our home gives us so much joy, it is a constant creative process and has taught us how capable we are of so many skills. When you have gardens, fruit trees, and a fixer-upper, you always have work, but it's pleasurable work that connects us to life and the Earth even right here in the middle of a neighborhood and a town buzzing around us.

If you would like to see how it looks to live on very little and thrive, learn all sorts of frugal ideas for cooking, cleaning, shopping, and living, please come visit me on my blog or my Channel.

Blog: *Katesinghsite.com*

YouTube: *Coffee with Kate*

Amazon: *Kate Singh*

Books by Kate Singh

The Homemade Housewife (lots of recipes and details)

Living on One Income (recipes and schedules)

The Green and Abundant Home (references and vegan recipes)

Queen of Penny Pinching (plenty of references at the end of the book)

Queen Housewife (recipes for homemade cleaners and beauty products)

And many more...

Other books to help on this journey of frugality

Americas Cheapest Family, Steve Economides

How to Cut Your Grocery Budget in Half, Steve Economides

The Complete Tightwad Gazette, Amy Dacyczyn

Sidetracked Home Executives, by Pam Young and Peggy Jones

Down to Earth, by Rhonda Hetzel

Bonus Chapter 7

Money saving tips I've learned over the years

Here are some fast tips that I've gone back to this year to save on money. Some may seem silly, but pennies add up to dollars!

Use wash clothes for dish rags

Grind coffee extra fine so you don't need as much and reuse pot for a few days by just adding a spoon or two of extra grounds each morning. It stretches the coffee.

Clothe diapers and nursing. Saves a ton of money.

Use the bed as a diaper changing station by laying out a towel each day and putting wipes and a small stack of diapers by it.

Get hair dye from Grocer Outlet. Mix a lighter and darker color and apply with a toothbrush to get the streaked look. Maybe have a friend help.

Paint only one wall as an accent wall to change a room. Find paint in the Oops section of paint stores or Home Depot for discounts. You may have to wait for a good color to be discarded.

Make curtains from sheets. You may find old antique lace bed covers or table clothes at a thrift store, and these make lovely curtains.

Cover an old couch with a sweet grannie knit blanket or quilt to cover the worn-out furniture piece. You can do this with a chair as well.

Repaint some of your furniture. You can make your own chalk paint. Watch *Olivia's Romantic House* for ideas. Or just use good spray paint.

Save seeds from produce you buy. There are tutorials on YouTube that will show you how to plant or save them. Bali just puts them in the soil. However, this doesn't work with all seeds.

You can grow food from the original plants, such as celery.

Use coffee or cooking oil cans as pots for your plants. Any large can is usable, but some are more attractive in a funky way. Old Asian sauce cans for example.

Have a box of powdered milk or canned milk in your pantry for cooking and baking.

Save all your jars from spaghetti sauce, jellies, peanut butter, especially those large Costco pickle jars. They make excellent storage jars when you start buying more bulk. The small baby food jars are handy for storing bulk spices and herbs.

Try putting 10% or more of the paycheck into savings.

Make your own candy and bake your own cakes for the family celebrations.

Stock up on turkeys after Thanksgiving.

Invest in a used deep freeze. I've found almost new for $100 on Craigslist.

Rent out a room. Do a background, work history, and credit check. Asked for references. Or ask around to find someone that has a good reputation and referred by a trusted friend.

Babysit on the side for extra money.

Buy a stove top percolator. You will never need filters and it will never break down.

Buy a stove top Italian espresso maker. These make the best coffee. I love my Café Bustelo espresso. Careful though, you may over clean after a cup.

Save big plastic containers for "homemade" Tupperware.

Go to your local Beauty School for haircuts, colors, manicures, pedicures, and facials for far less.

Try a high school play. So much cheaper than the local theater and more fun.

Go to a local high school basketball, football or baseball game.

Try the local hiking trails.

See what classes are offered at the Community Center.

Some theaters offer a summer pass for $1 movies once a week.

Only order off the dollar menus at fast food (They no longer have dollar, it's over a dollar or two dollar menus, but still cheaper).

Challenge yourself and family, make it fun and make it into a game.

Buy a gallon jug of vinegar. You can use in the kitchen for cooking, such as cakes and salad dressings, washing produce, and then use vinegar for making cleaners, washing windows, laundry softener.

Buy baking soda in bulk. It is used for cleaning and cooking as well.

Wash out the zip lock baggies and reuse many, many times.

Create a sewing box or tin and mend all the holes in clothing instead of throwing them away.

Always have powdered milk and creamer on hand for when you run out of the fresh stuff or for cooking.

Good luck!

Made in the USA
San Bernardino, CA
13 July 2019